INSECTS

Troll Associates

INSECTS

by Keith Brandt

Illustrated by Robin Brickman

Troll Associates

Library of Congress Cataloging in Publication Data

Brandt, Keith, (date)
  Insects.

    Summary: An introduction to insects, the class of
animals containing more than 800,000 kinds.
    1. Insects—Juvenile literature. [1. Insects]
I. Brickman, Robin, ill. II. Title.
QL467.2.B73   1984   595.7   84-2659
ISBN 0-8167-0184-9 (lib. bdg.)
ISBN 0-8167-0185-7 (pbk.)

You can find insects almost everywhere on Earth. Scientists who study insects have identified more than 800,000 different species, or kinds of insects. That's almost four times as many species as all other kinds of animals put together.

A fly is an insect. So is a beetle. So are ants and termites, butterflies and moths, wasps and bees, grasshoppers and fleas.

There are insects that live in the hottest jungles and in the driest deserts, on the highest mountains, and in the bitter cold of the Antarctic. There are insects that live on the surface of the ocean and deep in underground caves. There are even insects that live in vinegar! Others live in pools of oil, and still others spend part of their lives in salt beds.

All insects are small, when compared to most other animals. A giant-sized insect known as the Atlas moth has a wingspan of about twelve inches, or thirty centimeters. And some insects are so tiny that they are no bigger than a period at the end of a sentence. But most insects are about the size of your fingernail or a little bit larger.

This smallness has helped many species of insects to survive for many millions of years. It lets them crawl into a crack in stone or wood or behind a bit of leaf when an enemy comes close. And, being small, they do not need much food or water to stay alive.

9

All adult insects have certain things in common. They all have six legs, three on each side. Their bodies are divided into three sections: the head, the thorax, and the abdomen. The legs are always attached to the thorax. Digestion takes place mostly in the abdomen.

Almost all insects have a pair of feelers, also called antennae, growing from their heads. Most species of insects have wings. And some insects have extra feelers growing out of their abdomens.

Spiders are not insects. Spiders have eight legs instead of six, and their bodies are divided into just two parts, instead of three.

An insect has its skeleton on the outside of its body. It is called an exoskeleton, and it is made of a tough, hard substance called chitin. The exoskeleton protects the insect's body from injury and prevents it from drying out.

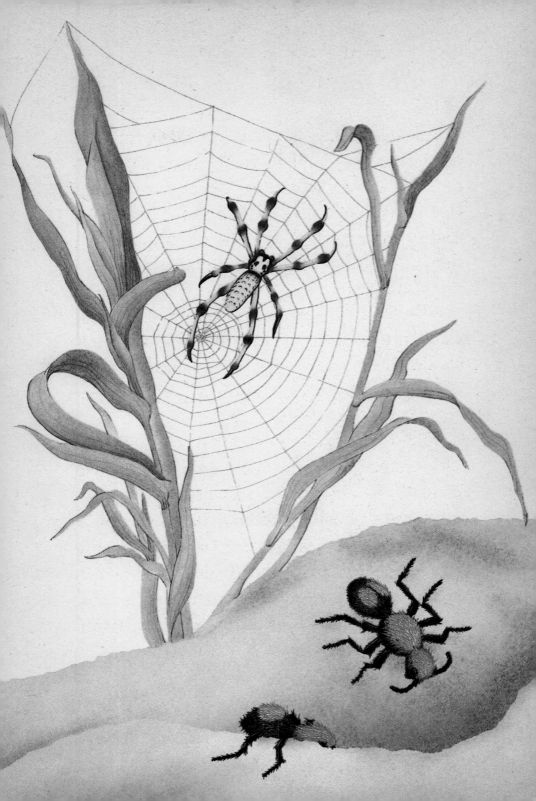

Most insects hatch from eggs. Some insect eggs are so tiny that you would need a magnifying glass to see them. Others are easy to see.

Each species of insect has different egg-laying habits. The mosquito lays a mass of eggs on the surface of water. The gypsy moth lays its eggs on the trunk and branches of trees. The ladybug, which is a kind of beetle, lays its eggs on a leaf. There are insects that lay one egg at a time, and others that lay thousands of eggs in a short period of time.

The eggs that are laid by a few insects, such as silverfish and springtails, will hatch into young that look just like their parents, only smaller. As they grow, they simply get bigger and bigger.

But most young insects do not look at all like their parents. They must change their form as they grow. This change in form is called *metamorphosis.* There are two kinds of metamorphosis—incomplete and complete.

Insects that go through incomplete metamorphosis are called *nymphs* when they hatch from their eggs. In some species, they resemble their parents, except that they have no wings. In other species, the nymphs look completely different.

As each nymph grows, it molts. This means its old shell cracks, and a new, larger one forms. With the last molt, the nymph becomes an adult. Grasshoppers and dragon-flies are examples of insects with this kind of metamorphosis.

Insects that undergo complete metamorphosis include butterflies and moths, flies and mosquitos, and bees and wasps. These insects have four stages in their lives. Like all other insects, the first stage is the egg stage. In the next stage, the insect is called a *larva*. It does not look at all like its parents.

The larva of a butterfly or moth, for example, is a caterpillar. It does nothing but eat, grow, and molt. When it is full-grown, it attaches itself to a leaf or the bark of a tree and goes into the next stage of metamorphosis. It becomes a *pupa*.

A pupa seems still and lifeless. But it is busy changing into an adult. In some species of insects, the pupal stage lasts just a few weeks. In others, it lasts through the winter. Finally, the shell or covering on the pupa cracks open, and the adult insect appears.

Life cycle of the monarch butterfly

Egg

L

Adult

Pupa

Its life span depends on its species. The mayfly, for example, lives just one day. The queen termite can live for a number of years. Many adult insects do not survive over the winter.

The main function of adult insects is to continue producing others of their species. To do this, they must lay eggs in a place that is safe from their enemies. It must also be a place that is close to food on which the newly hatched larvae will feed. This is why the gypsy moth lays her eggs on the bark of a tree, such as an oak. Gypsy moth larvae like to eat oak leaves, and as soon as they hatch they will find food nearby.

The adult gypsy moth doesn't eat anything at all, and it dies soon after its eggs are laid. Adult insects of other species do eat. Grasshoppers, crickets, and beetles eat leaves and other parts of plants. Plant lice, mosquitoes, and bees drink their food.

Bees sip nectar from flowers. Mosquitoes take blood from other living creatures. The praying mantis and the ladybug eat other insects. The cockroach eats soap, paper, plants, meat, glue, and almost anything else.

Insects that eat solid food have powerful jaws. Insects that take liquid food have a long sucking tube, like a straw. Other parts of insect bodies differ from species to species. Each eye of the housefly is really 4,000 tiny eyes, and certain dragonflies have 28,000 eyes on each side of their head. This kind of eye is called a compound eye.

Insects with compound eyes can see in almost all directions at once. But insects cannot see things more than two or three feet away. They also do not see colors as we do. For example, red looks black to a bee's eye.

Many insects also have a set of simple eyes, with one lens each, at the top of their heads. Entomologists think that these eyes do not see objects, but pick up movement and light only.

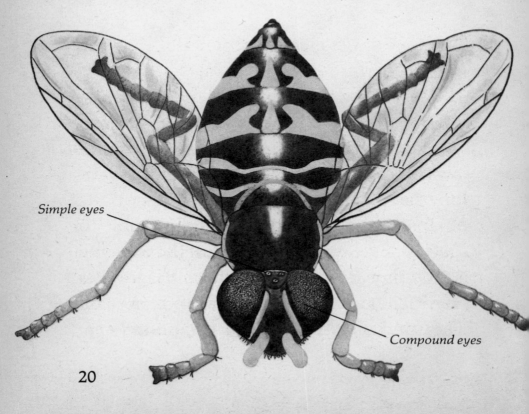

Simple eyes

Compound eyes

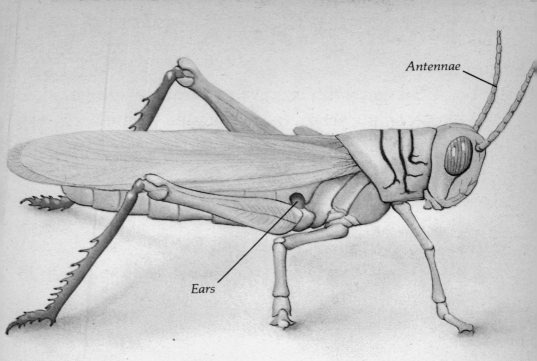

Antennae

Ears

Some insects have ears in their abdomens or legs. No insect has ears on its head. Insects also have no real voices. Those that make sounds do so by scraping their wings together, by rubbing one leg against another, or by rubbing their legs against their wings.

Insects get most of their information about the world through their antennae and body hairs. They take in smells through their antennae, and they receive other information through their body hairs.

Different insects have different ways to protect themselves from enemies. Some use camouflage. Many caterpillars look like tree twigs. There are moths that are almost invisible because their colors blend so well with the plants on which they rest.

Insects such as the bee, wasp, and hornet use their poisonous stings as defense. Others, such as the ant and the monarch butterfly, taste terrible to birds and most other insect-hunters. That is *their* protection.

The protection of the viceroy butterfly is that it fools its enemies. Although it does not taste terrible, it looks just like the bad-tasting monarch butterfly.

And, of course, flying insects escape from their enemies by swift flight. Dragonflies can go faster than thirty miles an hour, and hawk moths fly almost as fast.

Some insects, called solitary insects, live by themselves. Other insects, such as ants, termites, and most kinds of bees, are called social insects. They live together in colonies. Most ant colonies are underground. They are like apartment houses with many rooms connected by tunnels. Hornet colonies build large hives out of paper. Bees house their colonies in hives made of wax.

In most species of social insects, each member of the colony does only one job. Among bees, the majority of colony members are workers. There are a few drone bees, whose only job is to serve the queen. The queen usually lives four or five years and lays about half a million eggs in that time.

Termite and ant colonies are also made up of members doing certain jobs. Termites and ants have soldiers, workers, drones, and a queen.

Among solitary species, however, each insect must do all the jobs necessary to stay alive and continue the species. Sometimes solitary insects of the same species live near each other, but they do not work together.

Whether they are solitary or social, insects work very hard to survive. And many of them have great strength for their size. A bee can lift objects that are three hundred times its own weight. An ant can lift a stone more than fifty times heavier than itself. Grasshoppers are able to jump twenty times the length of their own bodies. And a tiny flea is able to leap eight inches straight up into the air. That would be the same as you jumping over a skyscraper.

Insects like the flea are a nuisance to people. Other insects can cause great damage. For example, termites attack wooden buildings. The larvae of gypsy moths destroy many trees every year. The larvae of clothes moths eat holes in woolen materials. There are beetles that damage fruit and vegetable crops, and weevils that destroy cotton crops.

There are also insects that cause serious diseases in people and animals. Certain mosquitoes carry malaria and yellow fever.

But there are many kinds of useful

insects. The brightly colored ladybug and the praying mantis eat harmful insects. The dragonfly eats mosquitoes. We get honey from honeybees and silk from silkworms.

But the most important job insects do for the world is pollination. As bees and butterflies go from flower to flower, seeking sweet nectar, they carry pollen on their bodies. If this did not happen, many flowering plants and fruit trees could not produce seeds. Among these are orange, apple, and pear trees, grapevines, blackberry bushes, and cotton plants.

In addition, millions and millions of insects become food for other animals, like birds, fish, frogs, and lizards.

Our world would be a much different place if all the insects suddenly disappeared. But we don't have to worry about that. In fact, even though scientists have already discovered over 800,000 different kinds of insects, they keep discovering more. They say there may be millions of new kinds out there—just waiting to be discovered.

Troll Associates

0-8167-0185-7